COUNTERPATH PRESS

OT

CHRISTINE HUME

Counterpath Press Denver, Colorado

www.counterpathpress.org

Copyright © 2010 by Christine Hume

Printed on acid-free, recycled paper

in the United States of America

Design and composition by Quemadura

Library of Congress Cataloging-in-Publication Data

Hume, Christine.

Shot / Christine Hume.

p. cm.

ISBN 978-1-933996-16-5 (pbk. : alk. paper)

I. Title.

PS3608.U44S56 2010

811'.6—dc22

2009028178

Distributed by Small Press Distribution

www.spdbooks.org

FOR JEFF AND JUNA WHO
REMADE MY NIGHT;
FOR MY ALLIES THROUGH IT,
CLAUDIA AND CHRISTINA

INCUBATORY 1

NOCTURNAL DIMENSIONS
OF THE FUTURE 13

SELF-STALKED 15

INDUCTION 16

LOOKING FOR A WORMHOLE 19

NOCTILUCENT ELEGY 20

SHRINES, DITCHES, BRIDGES 23

UM, UM ... 24

NIGHT IN YPSILANTI 26

SOME ARE BORN TO ENDLESS 27

MY ACTRESS 29

AMBIEN ANTHEM 30

CERTAINTY [VIBRATIONS OF
A BELL] FIDELITY 32

LIVELY DUB YOURSELF 34

SOMNILOQUY WITH INTERRUPTIONS 35

THANK YOU FOR THE FLOWERS 39

HAVOC ADDICT 40

INTERLUDE 42

NOT FOR YOU 46

NOBODY'S 47

MIRABILE DICTU 48

CONTINUATION ROOM 50

OBEDIENCE OF OPTICS 51

RADIO 54

I'M TALKING TO YOU 55

TRUST 62

APNEA 63

SOGGY MUFF 65

TELEMPATHY 66

ILLUSTRATION 68

FIELD OF SUSPICION 69

RECURRENT CURSE 72

BETWEEN THE WAY OUT
AND THE WAY HOME 73

CHARMER 78

LEASH 79

I EXHUME MYSELF 82

INCUBATORY

Are you comfortable?
                      I move inside night but am not its insides. I jerk and excise, I do not express. Outside is not made of the same dark as inside.

Can you open your eyes?

                          My looking does not bound back to me. It wanders further circles of eon in attempt to put the moon out of my moth-mind.

Can you hear my lullabies?

As when you descend into the ocean, you find yourself immersed in song; my whole body, made of water and umber, reverberates self-melodies.

What do you hear of our talk?
                    Blood fastens to all language at once, alive and
lying; all tongues lapping one another, dousing for routes into bodies.

Why do you kick at words?

To get your songs off my hands, I wade through their falls and uplifts. I dreamt a dog was trying to dig me out.

Why do you punch and undulate?

                                      I hear myself coming from your thoughts.

If I want to listen, I turn left; if I want to speak, I go right to bone.

Can you bear the sound of my voice?

                                         I place ears like traps on the amniotic shores. Past the hammer, past the bridge, past bellowing mares, past this cesspool, I go inward to check my traps.

Why are you lonely?

          From now on the noise you travel through will be my voice seeking you. It arranges my loneliness excruciating in twos. Pairs of anything become ears—the ones bound by shared mistake, the ones that won't work without you.

Are you lonely?

          Something shit on my shadow. My shadow sat on its stolen body.

How many senses grow from my fears?

                                      I know beyond doubt that electricity cannot steal the night from your organs. Your body's nocturamas are countless and okay. Except some skull pockets that burn without warning.

Will you raise your own kind?

Air woke up inside night, it ate away my tail. A slow pulse absorbed my gills. After that, I turned away from the dark, but felt it hot on my neck. I kept my nightshirt shut. I had to quarantine myself so as not to inherit its haunted rooms.

Where is the nutrient in it?

                        One third of your darkness reflects back. It listens to itself. Black syllables hatch. They flit into the tree. And again. Windwhipped hives, organizing.

What will leaving be like?

All I know fits through one night, down one hole, everywhere coming from all times until memory is mine. Forgetting inserts itself to the nth. Then it will become your clock, and birds will climb into your mirror.

NOCTURNAL DIMENSIONS OF THE FUTURE

Once I drew a line around myself, dug my shape into a rich field

Some night fell in, bruising itself

The fresh dirt was a muscle stowing away years

It wasn't dead, it just couldn't sleep

I stuffed night's hem into my mouth

Night also buttoned up when it couldn't find a thing to adorn

When it couldn't find a fly to swallow

If I keep my eyes quiet, if it mistakes me for blind

I dry heave fits of impure air

If I could retrieve that night from a dream

Its air wakes up amplifications inside my lungs

Shoveling scores the damage

When I wake back and forth for so long I can't remember

Being left or not being left alone, I fall bed to bed to bed

If I could move toward it while moving away

Night kills what it shifts into; I pine for where I alight

SELF-STALKED

I looked in all eight directions then spread out my tiger's skin. Before the public mind kicked in, I surveyed an inner shore. Its facets operated on me. I lost my lights and began my midnight thus: mental feet, mental lake, little mental pines, mental mile around the muzzle. I aimed my automatic at that outlandish organ hanging in the sky like a dazed stone. Its sea expression wet the evening; I captained the tempest there. Looking too long into the distant human pupil, I sharpened my harpoon. But my hands could not be organized. I wanted to tightrope up there on a mental binge. I reached for my quiver, my bird descended a failure one depth below time. The moment rotated, aggravated. Its color was extreme. In a heavy steel helmet, I matched that orb and tried to tackle it with a million mental muscles. The more I beat it, the more I couldn't see it. If I could turn it open like a glass knob, feel my way into its diamond cave. If I could tongue out its creamy mouth. If I could tickle it and bounce it on my knee. If I could dress it up. If it would fist me, if I could force it. The more I battered that moon, the more I could be it.

INDUCTION

Stitches and liquid morphine cannot keep it closed

Lunar halo runs circles more hollow than *forgot*

Steel birds fly from clocks

Striking the same hour in rounds

A freak disease tears across the vista

You've been told this is the year of medicine

Lunar halo must bother you tonight with some life

War shine and flare lit in the lips

The situation of radar gone deaf

A ring of unknown men waiting

To think of it is a tourniquet

Embracing you to the point to the point of

Sugar awake in the animal disaster

Vaccinations break and they bother you

The situation of its waves

Puts catheters in blather-mouths

Time for you to ride

Even when it acts hypnotic or botched

Tornado hanged in example

Eye sticking to its guns

It must bother you with oblong torment tonight

Between your deserts and escaped stars

Messes of radial spoils steal on you

Recognize your continuous tattoo

Lunar halo casts your face in harassments

It dissolves former weather in your ear

Takes up with your hexes

Ice becomes gas blasting into a foam hole

Out of which zodiac carcasses crawl

Under lunar halo, anyone who waits

For sleep waits to be seen to

LOOKING FOR A WORMHOLE

My first mind is night driving on and on. My blood evolved from this pitch and one night's tar accumulated in my mouth. If I go with my face made up, occult currents get plumbed. Their magnetic air is self-taught and not handled well. If I am fully in night, I cannot think ahead or use a song to get there. Night makes time by not remembering to go back. I make it mine by owning up to what I am not. Stars are swinging doors that miracle the shift. I am driving high into the taste of vanishing and starting points. Their arrows double-joint the dark. I am driving into my own eyes. Yellow lights pill the horizon hills. If I keep night to my right side, it ramifies until my solitudes splinter. My pulse stuck to the signal: *turnoverturnoverturn*.

NOCTILUCENT ELEGY

Walking yields the dangers of waiting

When you taste nowhere you can't return

You pass radio music muffled in a parked car

Wind does not stop burning down your night

It's a red noise like memory

Of wings circling the cliff

You pass a bandaged man with a sticky beard

This is not the face

You pass a couple burying themselves in sand

Your name called out

Won't make you look

Winds don't have names like oceans do

Slurring and drinking you double-ended

Drinking you over-present

Until your skin is itself a moon

Set against the black lapping

As magnetized as mute

Your heart-tick microphones

In every faceless thing

The wind moves around

Wind in the half-face of some future face

Grotto-boned boulder-sob

If you hear night

And it tells you it isn't

Falling then will you believe?

SHRINES, DITCHES, BRIDGES

[UNICA ZÜRN]

This night is a growing thing with its own mascara and lactation, its own ways of being hitched to two heavens. Each withdraws its wings. Eyesick, you leave ocellus there where you pressed your face— armpit, loin, sole of the foot, mouth, its intricate spit. You grow false nipples. Vulvas flash in a nest of lightning gates. Yet this night your existence depends on the doubt in a single pair of eyes stoning you from a low bridge.

UM, UM...

You may pound this night as much as you please

You will never pound into me what you think

You say the contrary, and the lashings madden

Night thinks you should pay for it

Pound at your belief until it's empty of you

Loaded with lords aft and boxes of forward lucifers

But how could a lucifer get fire in this crying hour

You could fill buckets with your drenched hems

No lightning rod will channel you

It will pound me better than a stormbird on its last wing

You pound this metal against my skull

Defang the dark's thunderstalk swerves

Words pound at me because I won't use them

Your lordish songs form obscure conduits

Night gnaws and unknots the anchor

Only to drag dark after me and lurk it in my orders

It pounds its meaning into me

That blankness packed with impressions I will not salvage

I endure the irate backpounding

Endure the obsessions that stand in for you

NIGHT IN YPSILANTI

Meet me at the old paper mill, come *parkour* and completely blank. Meet me at the graveyard where we'll sharpen to every sound. Meet me in state game-land with your foxtail and exit wound, with your earlobes and lungs and suntan. Meet me in the service elevator's broken surveillance. Meet me inscrutable in your prefab tragedy, nodding out in the needle garden, muffed in the dugout. Meet me under the water tower, head stuck in a starry bag. Meet me love at the money tree, in the burnt-out memory bank. Meet me in the revolving vows and be pushy; meet me in Piss Alley with your baby strapped in a stroller. Meet me at the Budget, in mirrors that double our medications. Straight away meet me in the planetary silence of skunk spray. In the keyed, jacked Olds backseat, ripped. Meet me in the razing highway lights, racing past in horror of what is about to occur; meet me fit for debauchery taught by Siouxsie. At the river banging and howling through town where we'll guzzle Red Bull. In silk and steel-tipped, meet me in the moth launch, at the radon hole. At the oil spill, fucked and covered up, un-unmovable at the "For Sale" sign, at the emergency shelter: meet my eye on your Imperial.

SOME ARE BORN TO ENDLESS

The lead body lies down with the feather body

If by memory foam, if on a dream-fast

Do not use a sleep mask because of your thoughts

Snuff out the count with an open mouth

Owls crowd out your words now

Let a wolf lope out of a word out of a fog

Let your night cape have a gas hole

Let the ocean uptake misshape your cover

Sleepers do not have feelings like real people do

You are not one of the guards

Even if guards do still exist

If your position is diagonal enough

A vortex rolls void full into you

Hasten to make use of that orbit

Emptying a nebula the way fatigue is

A way of worship if smashing waves

Do not listen for where the sound ends if

Smashing waves consolidate you then

Night never finishes even

As undertow takes the child think

Of each part of your body vanishing your

Skin as the dark that stares and stares back

MY ACTRESS

Costumed and impostured in her sheet, my actress cues hormonal ghosts with scheming cunts and sequin eyes. I won't be delivered silences like that. Tucked in, her arms are girls made of overwrought iron playing combat in the wet spot. Claque-dent down cold, I try dissolving her in sobs oozing from some blank world. I try nursing her grudges. I ruin her exhibits of caprice, but this one looks real breathing the curtain. She's pushing me down, unsatisfied. She breathes me to my own rank, where I'm waiting with weapons in my holes.

AMBIEN ANTHEM

Ghosts shove their heads through the moon

You shove yours through focal points

The future of your eye is its past

There is no sleep without a tall ghost lifting a small ghost up to see it

Your own eye lost in an oceanic moment

Dead spots and the line in knots

You and your mother at either end of an ancient static

Stereo guardians of the storm

Roll the mizzling movie

Ambush of blushes, deficits piled around the doghouse

The eye erasing a future eye

Each drains an attempt

An infinity you cannot stop infinity

Each moon each mother each cross-eyed ghost

Containers to be opened only in total darkness

Every eye falls down

The future of memory is a motherless force

In the pharmacy of amnesias

Sadness at having once slept through a meteor shower

CERTAINTY [VIBRATIONS OF A BELL] FIDELITY

Cat sleeps on her head like a nerve helmet. Several cataracts of blackness coming at once, torrents of rasp breaking her across a synapse gap. Hail pummeling the windows and the radio's whisper. When anyone asks what color her eyes are, she shrugs and says hazel. Cat would run away every night, through climates of frontier and incompletion. That must have been the very last night. She can walk back and forth like this for so long, in thought, in the hallway. If she closed her eyes, she could see more light than what's out there. Cat saw and didn't see what she passed: a bell tower striking. Cat could go anywhere, walk all night not going anywhere, for no one saw in the dark. Its arrowlike stillness, its vibe of dying lilac. Each step is into a bottomless pit, each step wakes a sleeping snake, each step collects poison at the hem. It is suddenly too late; she can no longer walk away. Cat saw and she didn't see her own body circling. In what direction do the lost veer? It is suddenly clear that she can no longer walk away. She can do what she likes, but she wants to be found. Cat buries the smell of her wine in the evening, the smell of her coffee in the morning. She checks the clock several times in the same minute, then dreams of her daughter mewing the door. It is not light that is failing, it's not light nor dark that dies. She grooms in that pigment, that drug.

LIVELY DUB YOURSELF

pigeons startle out
rubble and litter chimes

zeros nesting
in their pre-love

voice up through the drain
of a deep double sink

an ear is a gutter
for getting comfortable

SOMNILOQUY WITH INTERRUPTIONS

Every time we meet she says the exact same words the exact same way. I always sweat it because I am never coming from the same place.

    Losing deep face

One day I can feel my stomach and the next, where has it gone? She says get yourself out of that flesh suit.

    Losing it, broadcast exhaust

Sweat drenches my skin, but that doesn't make it mine. The tree in my knee is a mind of its own. I am the kind of tree that weeps.

    Grief-heavy
    Sweating distant views
    To outlast years

By her clock, I get the hang of my moodiness.

> *A blank beneath you brightened*
> *Like a net for falling into*
> *A hole in each memory grows*

My skin keeps weeping as if it were a window. Sky sticks to it. Always managing to be surprised by my own sweat.

> *Equator inside this inequator*
> *In a way you have already won*

That I can't see everything breathing all at once is part of the treatment. That I can't see sweat curdling my eyes. Unzip that sweaty woman suit. Step out of your own spoiled smell.

> *Breathing reveals invisibility*

If I pull open a drawer to reveal what I thought were love letters, I find an unposted gun.

> *Unresting sweat like sharks*
> *It's not as if thoughts were tropical fish*

Can you hear it? She does not ask if I can. My ears are filling with tears. I'm afraid my body won't fight for me against thinking

> *How will I get you to stop*
> *Let me help you with that gun*
> *A tiger licks me everywhere his roar*

is pure treatment. Given the choice to have no choice.

> *You won't even*
> *Remember this part tomorrow she says*

New sweat marks only crotch and cleavage, unselves my self-love. I could become myself again. She says, don't think, come to yourself all at once from the future. I could be one of three people I might turn back into.

> *Let it out let it out let it out or*
> *Sweating is begging*
> *Sweating is confessing*
> *left out   let me out*

Breathing is a form of waiting. I cry it out. Nail my foot to the ground, she says as if someone were trying to steal it.

Breathe into your dead man
As if you were dying

She says I have no kneel in me. Breathe into my doubt as if it were an injury.

As if it were infinitely dead swarming over dead faces

THANK YOU FOR THE FLOWERS

Flustered buttercups blown loud, yellows of dry crying locust wings. They woke me when they bloomed. Pinks fully open and the hour behind remorse busts forth. This arrangement feeds on dark so that my eyes will die opening. Orange crawls my skin; it narcotically ticks in my nose. Orange advances Earth's roundness while the reds' musty stacks are hard to read. They come like a quote of something not said, they come verbatim, shedding whole oxygen bodies in this small room. Their explosions embed our bed with broken teeth. Threesomes of coxcomb bite me rural. Their touchy hoods will dry, close, fade, but never quite die. Saffrons and fawns give a lily shape to your carnations. There are sprays of violets put right. I try to imagine you picking them for me one strenuous limb at a time. The joy that rose up their stems when cut! The joy that knots at the top, stuck there, is a color too big to swallow. I'm dangling in that display, feelers floating out for the rest of the accident. It is meant for me. You expect to find my answer in their cheerfulness, by your own florid traces. Yet to go in and out without a scent is impossible. Take my hand and get me into the argument.

HAVOC ADDICT

You still have
your tailbone

and bits of riffs
you pick at

you still have
universal

fornifications in a
recurring tool shed

though your dangers
have clammed up

their fatidic transmissions
make you suffer

snakes every night
a bitch barks

at a blue comet: but
what's the matter

will no longer
devour you.

INTERLUDE

Wandering clotted woods, you come to a shadowy compound of human organization. Here is a territory between first and second sleep, full of dusk mutter.

MOTHER ESTROGEN: The ultrasound picks up a luminous moon in this gray, grainy corner.

MOTHER BROKER: Looks like an owl killed by lightning.

MOTHER-IN-THE-TREES: An owl reshapes its face to shove a new sound down its ear. When you dream, you do the same. Your face reforms so that you may experience the next day.

MOTHERNUT: I am thinking up names for my new face.

MOTHER-IN-VISUAL-PURPLE: My paint can is almost empty, but I am still listening for names to spray on the bridge.

BORROWED MOTHER: What, so that they can have a good look at you? Are you listening through a pipe?

MOTHER ESTROGEN: I'm listening through a bossy womb with my extra night-finger.

ROGUE MOTHER: Think back to the way it used to be. With a stick on your shoulder carrying a canary in an opal cage. Not even an owl saw the open then.

MOTHER MADDER: Don't let them seal up childhood with their invisible tape.

MOTHER CLAUSTRAL: The blind years of limbo, burning and hovering like verdurous day-glo moths.

PROSTHETIC MOTHER: Even if you could have said those words in the daytime, no one could hear them.

MOTHER-OF-CAGED-AROMAS: Run amok with self-pity and catch restless legs. Sleep in self-pity or awaken in fatigue. Realize that fatigue is an awakening trance. Wake up what you are saying.

MOTHER-IN-THE-TREES: If I want to break habit, I'll wake in the uncanniest room of all—my body asleep.

COLD-MOTHER-PLUNDER: Lady, save me from my own buzzsaw and amnesiac fever sleep.

MOTHER FERUS: But what if sleep were the parasite? Not these names, which like dreams simply domesticate sleep. What if sleep were the thing with fangs?

MOTHER CONFUSION: In my mouth, doubt incubates each name I host. Doubts won't dissolve like aspirin in the total darkness. Yet in the dark, my voice saying her name has no hidden face.

MOTHER ESTROGEN: This is the tired stuttering I refuse to love. This tired defect is tired and what tired begets is a tinderbox of ancient rage.

MOTHER BROKER: Don't mistake remembering for seeing. Don't mistake inquiry for love.

MOTHER TOMORROW: Crypto-negation is the sky's soft chewy spot.

MOTHER DIAZEAPAM: What will it be like when the fontanel closes for good?

MOTHER DEFECT: It will beat waking up with fists we can't uncurl. Right now we can't even seem to enter twilight.

MOTHER CONFUSION: If I lied more, could I remain perfectly faithful to sleep?

MOTHER TOMORROW: Our job is to survey past sleep, not to promote vestigial sleep or usher it into the future.

BORROWED MOTHER: Then tell me who slept up all the sleep there is? And left us with only dead time.

COLD-MOTHER-PLUNDER: Creatural sieve! I can hear the raw wind nursing your sores.

MOTHER-IN-THE-TREES: Are you hormone-drunk? Cut it and drink what's left of what you think. Here, catch yourself becoming what you are no longer.

MOTHER FERUS: Makes my head cash red.

MOTHER-OF-DOGS: Owl chronocrafts a certain tone so moonlight won't trap you. Names from another woods exchange one for one. Hear them?

MOTHER MADDER: Revealing the sudden ugliness of everyone upright.

NOT FOR YOU

When nicotine was in a tree
it needled me
It set suspicion
on whatever I conceived
Birds blackening
their backtalk

That night came up
from a well
It deepened itself
by emerging
like two stones
put in my hands
to fasten to sleep

That bottomless night
thawing and spilling out
      "I…I…"
give you my hand
like an amputee
feeling for a match

NOBODY'S

As if life were going on night after idiot night its tint childrening voids fast through salt air all the same dark as every yard between our faces and stars motoring in clean hammergait at the axis is a drain we are looking for in our boat guided only by dark helixed around nerve a double rung to nothing but fuck-ups growing over satellites we confuse with vows aloud like a foghorn dampening a deep shade of speed that parts us then departs toward dark amped by the wind which is sick tonight gunning its familiar manias in the boat blitzing to an island where desire is a lack looking in all directions within a mirror held up to cure a fear of enchantment on the eve of a reunion already stretched thin picking up its gallopbark our blood wants to evaporate the ancient it circulates in order to find a morning cornered and funneled into the shape of a woman who wakes on a boat thinking she has edged up on for once landed its clairvoyance and goes on

MIRABILE DICTU

Your sleep-eye has
its irreversible reasons

its ocean closes
and closes

He digs markers
out of a graveyard

to make way
for an interstate

A dog leads
you home that night

When the dog is done
licking your face

you'll know that
the graveyard

looks back
putting circles

under your eyes
You thought he

wanted to be seen
You thought you

thought when you tire
of night stuck

full of eyes
go with him

and he'll start
you from the start

CONTINUATION ROOM

Expect bewitched frequencies : a tongue to be there : bees bedded in what we said : yellow pulls across the ceiling : twice sensitized : daisy inside the bedside clock : tangent touches : flare at the window : one greening itself

Doze off blind-stripped : your spine gives off flies : plumbing the null room : a yellow robe mouths the doorknob : shadow-eyes seizure : string of tides : magnet-had and stabbed through : two crucial hues drench each other

Suspend the sun by our voices : neck deep in purkinje shifting : queen deep in knees : we fox our green cases : face to face frictions : buried alive : twenty-five electric corrections : a splinter-listening requires us : listen twice

Lock limedusk in bull-light : picked by promise : sweatwilds wake in your idle clavicle : head emptying loud oceans : a self-drawing face repeats : eyes' allergic circuit : varicose chandelier : murder of worms on a limb

OBEDIENCE OF OPTICS

Law speaks of
a girl who bled

from her eye
until it turned

itself in and
cannibalized sight

Girl raised one good
and one bad eye

their rivalry glimmered
glaucoma off-gassing

She looked out
the bus window

ossifying the irides
Her downtown eye

didn't shut so
got moon-blinded

Another was
plucked by a magpie

then a bee sting
on the lid fattened

a second chance
Looking at lightning

stole its clarity
words stared

into their opposites
Eyeball outgrown its lid

Girl threw down
all her Accusers

in the trembling grass
at the Examiner's feet

A slut-eye
then lived illegally

in her navel
like a peephole

only trusting
what it saw on the sly

RADIO

To explain aspiration. Explain the transmissions. You play at alienation. As if to explain relations. Gather strangers wearing pajamas. Cut the lamp. Explain in flame and caffeinated. In natal anguish. To explain a lack of harmony. By savoring vaccinations. Astral tattoos going astray. To explain a galaxy. Back out of range. Have a laughing accident. In wasted watts. Explain your absence. By flaking out. Explain octane and octave. With static waves. Basaltic layers of amaze. In a stranger's bed. Explain in accent. An antenna's range for romance. In chilblains. In shattered rays. To explain the channels. Rake each other's hair. Ward off the animal again. Explain strangers. By trafficking in apparitions. You hazard the rain with a vacant stare. To explain accuracy. When one chants to a star. Your chances amp up. Many accidents about to be played. You stalk explanations. Bank on anger. Atlases of slain confidence. Explain slapping back and the attempts. A bat trapped in the attic. Radar in the maple. One sabotaged face. At the station. To stay grateful. Unravel the signal. To explain the air burial. Explain what you say after dark. After you came to in an alley. Having unbraided a stranger's dreams.

I'M TALKING TO YOU

[TO BE READ SILENTLY BESIDE A SLEEPING PERSON]

Night sweats are evidence
of teeth puked and baked
into cakes like razors,
of fireflies bearding your mouth
sticky after slugs of rotgut,
of dinofelis in sleep debt,
of howls shoving themselves
down your throat—what
you have counseled me to do
I have not done.

My hands started barking unexpectedly
there was no way to quiet the other thing
that mouthful of deforming
circulated its volume
I moved in this irradiated air like a mobile
my heart had a red ear
my voice knotted
my voice was a tentacle more sensitive than I could bear
I could not stop being aware
so help me   so halve you
my hands were gongs
my hands were pillows held to that echo hole

After blue, auto-history kicks in
after hours, you chew out the sheriff's meaty face
after eaten out comes heart
after empty, a snapshot
after inexistence, believe me
      snatch is a stud-hammer
      casting off consolations
after god, a second time don't hurt
after thank you, an inability to speak

Up by my feet
quick to be raised
onto soldier's shoulder's
to see what was better—
to belong to both
or to marry one—
overhead a robin replies:
to be shot in the woods

Tell me again the story
of why you lied, why there is no one
you cannot do something for.
Medicine and makeup crowd the table,
every hour hits its midnight—
isn't it just like you to be quiet
when I'm trying to hear things

Some rustic understood my childhood
that pleasure of infinite objection, ob-
jection, infidelity to doubt, crushed err
when night endured without my face
and unfit fingers locked me out of my head
resting on a red weathered pillow.
You were the voice of a river fiddle
wafting to my idle auspicious inland.

You bite my tender mind
you go back and forth
in a forestall of fever trees
sorrowful as new fire
finishing in my fault anyway

Once you're in love
learn a dull blundering purpose
pulling above and below
do you see how it works
I speak to you (listen)
you speak to me (listen)

TRUST

Each morning light corridors your infinite bones. The intrigues end at the edge of hemlock. A spell awakens, an ear is awakening. You wake to murmur and a warm grazing hand. Clouds of fur shine from the corners, its aches and its things kept awake. Night doesn't wait to be hunted; it hides in corners. You shake the shape of your own thought: a glow around doors, bat in the attic being born. You wake to traces of your own mattering. Years later you awaken in a truck snoring the mountain bends. You open your eyes under foggy omissions. Feel what the light thinks at its very nape. There, you wake the struggle between danger and duration. You attempt to awaken by storming your solitude. By sleeping in strange rooms. A throb vowels your mouth. You wake even if it changes nothing. Even as it fails.

APNEA

Stop at the window
Your thoughts are rabid
Outside one man is often a wolf
To another sweating in the meadow
Stop in limbic welter
Evolving wolves bloom
Your long thoughts heave
And lengthen on the long grass
Bulldoze down the hill stop
Take the goodbye out
To the river and its branch
Its curses slipping
On god knows nothing
Full grown through the thicket
Come through for me stop
This once at the thicket
More ticked than faced, choked up
At the window bolted out of your weather
Wolves despise a window

They overcouple themselves
Downriver murky hair
Whips over rocks
Stop at the mood of rocks in dusk
What do you mean you're alone
Goddamn wolves
The sopping grass restirs
Its smell and stops
At the river two bodies wide
A dream of seeing through one eye

SOGGY MUFF

I'll not wake, I'll not be wailed : I'll sleep suddenly in your tower : I'll sleep south through your France in a second skin : I'll be my own superior comforter : crunk-dumb and crusty : I'll not wake purring, ruby-throated : not with a tornado in my lap : not at docks nor in the spas : I'll never wake feeling along night-bloomers : will not stop spindling for cocked wet lamps : I'll not in your blazing blazon : I'll never wake slaked in unruly rooms : not frisked in your miniatures : not flayed on a maculate angle : I'll not wake bipedal in a rabbit suit : not in a lab coat or on a black pony : I'll not hear my name and be brought to :

TELEMPATHY

I owe it to the meat of clones to feel when doubles stag

I hole up with the hare baboon and bleat when trouble sprays

I hawkeye the hung raccoon who freaks when stumble speaks

I order two above the floor and creep when tongue's in pain

Werewolf werewatch the muzzle in the ugh comes here comes the hum

Hussy fur underneath the contiguous home unsmuts itself alone

I suffer by the hide again to pulse the wretched gash

I soft up to harpoon wails to watch a young buck agitate

I shot my dove's scruple score when humped a mawkish grave

I vote it to the fetus meat to lick white neck remains

My ovary's fat plunder mocks when marsupial awakes

I owe it to the bush of flies to tell when fuckers prey

ILLUSTRATION

Back turns up its volume : erects a fence to disembowel words : offers an over-groped pelt : wild black ferns : competitive weather patterns : in electromagnetic currents : around the armpit : curve of alert armor : brute and bent : double-fathered joints : raw jawing nicorette : to hell with this sweaty meat : pent melatonin : blue-wired hips : legs lying perdu in rural quarters : toes like shattered icicles : omens vex the bones : iron glove for forgeries of touch : slapped down the spine : an ass-hatch that's dropped a screw : guttered ordure far and near : starlight grips the shoulder blades in silver fists : rippling as if they were eyelids : closed over dreaming eyes : closed but drowning the birds : flying to him : one by one : hollow-boned beneath his hand : a hummingbird's heartbeat : let one through a supernal trapdoor : just try to find him : try to cross to find out : look through the verge : stay back and let the lost find you

FIELD OF SUSPICION

eyes on water

eye was weather

stole back feathers

that ides—half-lied

to the flirt

his white shirt

rides a tree

onshore a virus

twice hidden in

spiral vision

involved you

unto inversion

you eyed it

wild in exact

flight written

inside you another

sickle sun

sharpening pitch

on intuition

cricket-insistent

wind infected

five eye hives

in his tree was electric

wait you

waste *why*

when you

could have

caught sight

RECURRENT CURSE

not in the grove or the pond : not atop iris hill : sticks and steps along the wet street : you follow the Setter : keep highway light to your right : find the gravel drive : a voice in blinkless phlox : aging in the mailbox : its menace recognizes you : pick the yellows : store your teeth in the brickwork : find a battery in the yard : piss in the hedges : near where the furniture is buried : damned rash on the front porch : electrical drone : pretend it was never yours : put your face in the window and let it dirty : see that you are not required : riddled with niches : trawl all the attics : oil and acid stained : even if the Setter reverses his course : a ghost is to pursue : go through the door : one of nineteen doors : panic at the argyle wallpaper : its faint warble : crave a cigarette : no one will say you can't sleep here : squirrel nest in the ceiling fan : the closet's dead cord : fifteen windows : each sun you strangled : tic tic brutish tic : on the mantle a defaced painting : cobwebs rotting corners : what won't get said : won't change what you are : mangled spiral staircase : up there and not permitted to leave : up there and not

BETWEEN THE WAY OUT AND THE WAY HOME

Circle of stringed instruments around us

Two faces of a mountain

Somewhere between, a shortcut

I have not been permitted

Dumb as dark, dark as blunt

Stars pulled life-sized into bed

Stairs draw you down to the river

Night steeps you in a need to move

Chant of feet behind you

Moth-like lights in your mouth

Taste of tungsten and fungus

You know the river will carry whatever you throw in

Impossible to draw to scale that conversation

One bridge black as tangled

Black neck of it sweating stars

Swallows diving into barren water

Someone is always standing on the bridge

One by one your expressions surface

Deep black pouring waxen faces

Look up at a face painted on rock

Black as cashmere black as black

Coming out of your icy throat

Once from mid-river I yelled "decide!"

Another time I heard everything you ever said

Vague glitter of electrochemical lapses

One consequence of being touched

Its echo is your name and its re-echo *au secours*

One note from a bird, one note of apology

Black river burning off acetaminophen

From forehead to eddy, it hurts

Stand in it mauled, and withered, knowing

Something in the water cannot be calmed

Tin and iron smiles flicker across it, rotted moods

Once I couldn't get out of my own clutch

And the dark reshaped my eyes

All eyes begin in the night and are full of it

Black as sham, as well-oiled laughing machines

When you leave, your memory sinks in the river

One by one your eyes return to alphabetic river stones

They reattach themselves to my throat

Your reflection in the slants and stammers

Black as the one night I want

The night I want to bring back alive

Once I heard you washing the river

As if it were a person dislodged full-real from the mud

Roving sullen things cough on the bank

Streetlights pick at the remains

The town is gone, wept, mutilated

Blood knocking in your arms almost makes them float

CHARMER

His eye sweats down : to its magnet : drawn to small holes : he siphons catacombed crabs : from exits in the sand : tricks out a buried cur : eye-arrowed and blood-drawn : carried by mesmerized bees : opens its petals well

Lures out the tail : his sum of come-ons : play the empathies' sinews : until it cannot suffer away from him : he leeches off its memory : cuts an emergency gut : coaxes out parasites : mites from saliva : an apology pulled from molars : it is dirty he says

And rolls clouds into his eyes : summoning another stray : out of outlandish dunes : this one empties almost too easily : his adrenalin evacuates an anxious dream : larks nesting in its eye sockets : watching what you say : but cannot say yourself

LEASH

Tongue heard tell of your enterprise.
Tore loose from turning skies.
Convolutions got it bound.
Migrating heart of a hound.

Shaped by conflicting doubts.
Let out moldy idiom, spat a cloud.
Tongue broke into ten thousand
Severed-tongue demands.

Tongue went down south.
Put itself in a goat's mouth.
Making words reek and public.
If only Tongue wouldn't suck dick.

If only Nerve would rise up to the past.
If only Tongue swallowed the said.
No comfort in that marriage bed.
Myclonic jerks are going fast.

Listen to the succubus in camouflage.
Tongue trades in sabotage.
Switch pulled from cockeyed pines.
Strike rural and set it afire.

Ear-deepening dark flashes and seeds.
Tongue burrowed a hole for feces.
Crack it if you want to see yourself.
Your daughter beasting out.

Bird-nerves stirring up the yard.
Children who won't be sorry.
Knew it was alive because you beat it.
Tongue growing a new tip and ornery.

Talking as if crying or tripped.
Conveyed a voice you couldn't isolate.
Lemurs, June bugs, goatsuckers, guns give lip.
Where were you out so late.

Lash it, hold it, tie it, bite it, cut it out.
Tongue's time has come.
It has come to in a fit of laughter.
Finds you hanging from the rafters.

The mothers and fuckers are padlocked in blue.
Tongue has no one to talk to.
But the answer is no I do.
Love you, and love you.

I EXHUME MYSELF

When we sleep in the barn under thirty heavy blankets, I am never coming back.

I sleep naked with a knife in the down.

A knife is too short to stab any vital thing.

The night we met, my eyes no longer cut me in two.

I grew knives and slept on them, expanding.

I grow weak eyes where the knives had been.

From the ceiling I stared at, vertigo spilled down, hid, ripped into mind.

Waiting for morning is not the same as sleeping.

A dream is a naked idea snapped awake.

The backward splashes of your feet running through rain.

Singing bye-bye baby gauntling, Daddy's gone drinking.

(You are not there where I have looked.)

When I raise the manhole lid, I am dead on my feet.

None of the babies come out alive.

When you come home with a live bat in your hands.

I look for a window, but go under the sheets.

I could never sleep at the back of my mind.

Dreaming is a blindness that looks back.

Walking out from a dream in the wrong direction.

Under an electric blanket on high in August.

Crawl into a bad dream backward over dirt to find a way home.

The whole family jerks awake realizing we are coverless.

Love rips into mind, hides in its own smoke.

Wait in the dark for your mother to return.

Walk into a dream where wires cry you out.

When each night waking leaks a new ghost.

When I woke in the unadulterated dark of our car.

I woke bombing inside the race dream.

Awakened, but not yet there.

When night pushes me down its huge eyeball.

Everything apt inches toward failure.

My eyes grow backward to replace the future.

Your mother insists we take her high, stiff bed.

The ceiling crack's habit of looking like a rabbit.

Walk with me out of the evisceration dream.

False moons swerving.

Can you turn them out?

Light twisted tight like a sheet.

When fog invades my leaving-you dream.

I stick my finger down night's throat.

We paint the bedroom Bird of Paradise.

In the hotel bed's bleach-stench, staring at the ceiling.

You see the same things no matter what is in front of you.

Three-chambered synaptic headless moons.

You don't know the half of it.

You were outside hanging all the moon's faces: kicked out, tensile, tricked, eclipsed.

The goathead eyes photos of the dead.

When you wake, I am asleep and digging at my own throat.

In the day you say one thing, in the night you own another.

You say, look out the window.

And years later we go back, stand there.

Look at what you have given up to be with me.

I wake with red scratches on my neck.

I tell you I am in love.

You tell me you know.

But what you know is something else.

Marks like tracks down my neck.

I don't root down into your dream.

I will not dig a fetus out of my throat.

My hands will never find it.

Digging a pit like it was something else, and singing.

Both of us stare at the same ceiling.

You explain this to me.

I almost disappear when I am in the pit.

Morning comes in the middle of night.

We dig at something lodged there.

I wake up missing want.

Grateful acknowledgment is made to Eastern Michigan University for its support, as well as to the editors of the following journals and books where the poems here first appeared: 12×12, *Aufgabe*, *American Letters and Commentary*, *Aphrodite of the Spangled Mind*, *Black Clock*, *Boston Review*, *Caffeine Destiny*, *Canary*, *Coconut*, *Columbia Poetry Review*, *Colorado Review*, *Culture Vulture*, *Damn the Ceasars*, *Del Sol Review*, *Denver Quarterly*, *Electronic Poetry Review*, *Emprise Review*, *Esther Press*, *Fence*, *Filter*, *LIT*, *The Literary Review*, *LVNG*, *Mark(s)zine*, *Not for Mothers Only: Contemporary Poems on Child-Getting and Child-Rearing*, *Opus 42*, *Parakeet*, *The Pulchritudinous Review*, *Sonora Review*, *St. Petersburg Review*, *Traffic*, *Typo*, *Verse*, *Western Humanities Review*, and *Women's Studies Quarterly*.

Christine Hume is the author of *Musca Domestica* and *Alaskaphrenia*, as well as a chapbook with CD entitled *Lullaby: Speculations on the First Active Sense*. She teaches in and directs the interdisciplinary Creative Writing Program at Eastern Michigan University, where she hosts *Poetry Radio*, a radio show/podcast available through iTunesU. She lives in Ypsilanti, Michigan with her partner, Jeff Clark, and their daughter, Juna.